What Do We Stand For?

"This book is an important resource in understanding the ideological, philosophical, and spiritual dimensions of the war against Islamic jihadism." **Dr. Sebastian Gorka,** Vice President & Professor of Strategy and Irregular Warfare at Institute of World Politics and author of *Defeating Jihad*

Also by Larkin Spivey

God in the Trenches
Miracles of the American Revolution
Battlefields and Blessings: Stories of Faith and Courage from World War II
Stories of Faith and Courage from the Korean War
Stories of Faith and Courage from the Vietnam War
A Skeptic's Guide to God
A Skeptic's Guide to God Group Study

What Do We Stand For?

AMERICAN IDEALS IN THE WAR
AGAINST ISLAMIC JIHAD

Larkin Spivey

To Lani

She has always known what she stands for.

Contents

Acknowledgments

I am grateful to Dr. Sebastian Gorka, John Guandolo, Philip Haney, and Dr. Nicolas Papanicolaou for their support. These distinguished Americans have dedicated their careers to serving America and have published influential works to educate their fellow countrymen about the threat of Islamic jihadism. They have allowed me to feature their books and biographies in Appendix II to this book to better inform readers about the nature of this threat.

My wife, Lani, has spent a lifetime standing tall for her family and her country and has contributed extensively to this book. I have been inspired by her efforts over the years to support our active-duty military and veterans through her fund-raising efforts and involvement with Fisher House and Franklin Graham's Heal Our Patriots.

I am also grateful to the staff of the US Naval War College Library in Newport, Rhode Island, especially Julie Zecher and Gina Brown. Their good nature and professionalism have been of immeasurable value to me for many years, contributing to my research for this book and all my others. Also, the expertise and insights of Dr. William Morrill were extremely helpful in the formative stages of this book's development.

INTRODUCTION
Do We Stand for Anything?

You may have heard the expression: *"If you don't stand for something, you will fall for anything."* A *Wall Street Journal* editorial explains the apparent inability of the European nations to face the threat of radical Islam by rephrasing the dictum as follows: *"People who believe in nothing, including themselves, will ultimately submit to anything."*[1] These words go to the heart of a serious problem. The fact that Europe is experiencing an escalating crisis becomes more obvious every day. Since 2014, over two million refugees have flooded the continent, 70 percent of whom are young men.[2] Europol, the European Union's law-enforcement agency, reported in February 2016 that 130,000 male refugees in Germany were missing from refugee centers and presumed to be involved in illegal activity.[3] The refugee influx is also known to harbor large numbers of Islamic State opera-tives.[4] Not surprisingly, terrorist attacks are occurring with increased frequency, aimed at major cities in the heart of Europe.

In response to this crisis, European leaders are mired in uncertainty. Tolerance is an important Western value, and the plight of refugees is looked upon sympatheti-cally. However, few were prepared for this tidal wave of humanity with completely different lifestyles and be-liefs. Although everyone abhors the violence of terrorist attacks, the underlying, long-term threat to Europe lies with the masses of displaced people who will likely nev-er assimilate into the cultures of their European hosts. These masses also harbor the ideologues seeking ac-tively to undermine those cultures. Everyone is against violence, but European culture is being overwhelmed as Europeans themselves seem to lack belief in anything to stand for in a positive sense. Unfortunately, this descrip-tion could be applied to much of the American popula-tion as well.

By now we know that there are people in various parts of the world who intend to cause great harm to western civilization. In fact, war was overtly declared on America on September 11, 2001, by Islamic radicals who flew airplanes into our buildings. Our military and law-enforcement establishments have been engaged in this conflict at home and abroad ever since. These efforts to fight violence are vital and necessary but in themselves are inadequate to counter the kind of threat our nation is facing now.

Even though violence is the outward face of this enemy, the long-term threat to America is the same as that to Europe. There are Islamic radicals in America with an ideological agenda opposed to our way of life. More are being trained and are arriving daily in our midst. We have to be prepared to fight the violence that we know is coming. However, there are also ideological, philosophical, and even spiritual dimensions to the conflict that have to be acknowledged and where the battle must be fought.

Islamic jihadists have demonstrated their willingness to strive for their world vision for as long as it takes and to die for it, if necessary. Is there anything so compelling for Americans? Is there anything we would die for, or even stand up for? Every American must answer this question and consider for him or herself what about our nation is worthy of support and even devotion. Clear and strong answers will be the only counter to the challenges that lie ahead to the system of government and way of life that we cherish.

1 Bret Stephens, "Is Europe Helpless?" *Wall Street Journal*, Page A13, July 26, 2016.

2 Yousef Bodansky, "The Jihad Escalates in Europe," *Defense and Foreign Affairs Strategic Policy* 44, no. 5/6 (2016): 4–9. *Military and Government Collection*, EBSCO host, accessed September 16, 2016.

3 Ibid.

4 Ibid.

CHAPTER 1
Radical Islam

By the literal meaning of its name, we know that Islam is a religious/political system of submission—to Allah and to religious authority. In its earliest history it was spread by conquest, through the Arabian Peninsula, across North Africa, and into Europe until forcibly stopped by greater military power. Its founder and warrior-prophet, Muhammad, was succeeded by a line of caliphates who ruled major parts of the Islamic world until the fall of the Ottoman Empire after World War I. The postwar government of Turkey sought to secularize the nation by banning the public practice of religion and by disbanding the seven-hundred-year-old caliphate.

As the Middle East was carved up by the victorious European powers after World War I, Muslims found

1

themselves leaderless and marginalized to a greater extent than ever before. Recognizing this void, an Egyptian cleric named Hassan al Banna established an organization called the Muslim Brotherhood in 1928 with the express purpose of unifying Islam by reestablishing the caliphate and the rule of Islamic law in Egypt and beyond. Within a decade it had grown internationally to over a half a million members.[1] By the time the Brotherhood came to America in the 1950s, it consisted of hundreds of branches in dozens of countries.

Other than its founder, the Muslim Brotherhood's greatest ideologue was a man named Sayyid Qutb, called by many the "Intellectual Godfather" of the Brotherhood[2] and of the present-day Islamist movement.[3] Qutb was an Egyptian who had come to America in 1948 to study and returned home to join the Muslim Brotherhood as a writer on social and religious issues.[4] His most influential work is a book titled *Milestones,* published in 1964. In it he reasserted what he considered the traditional and proper focus of Islam and the necessity of *jihad*:

> *Islam is the way of life ordained by Allah for all mankind...and orders practical life in all its daily details.*

Jihaad in Islam is simply a name for striving to make this system of life dominant in the world.[5]

Phrases such as "dominant in the world," "leader of mankind," and "world leadership" recur often in the book, referring to the ultimate goal that the entire world be brought under Islam and the laws that derive from the Koran, known as shari'a.[6] Qutb describes how part of the Koran was written in Muhammad's early peaceful years in Mecca and other parts later in Medina. As the Koran was revealed in stages, the more violent later verses were considered to supersede or abrogate the earlier. Explaining the so-called peace verses of the Meccan period, Qutb states: *"When Allah restrained Muslims from jihaad for a certain period, it was a question of strategy rather than of principle."*[7] Stating Allah's true principle found in the later verses, he explained,

All the verses of the Qur'an (Koran) in which victory is promised, or in which spoils are mentioned or where it is told that the polytheists will be punished in this world by the hands of the Believers, were revealed in Medina... Other societies do not give it (Islam) any opportunity to organize its followers according to its own method, and hence it is the duty of Islam to annihilate all such systems.[8]

If these views of Islam seem far removed from the main-stream, another perspective is available from the early days of the American republic. When Thomas Jefferson inquired of the ambassador from Tripoli by what right his nation was attacking American ships, the ambassa-dor replied that Islam: *"...was founded on the Laws of their Prophet, that it was written in their Qur'an, that all nations who should not have acknowledged their authority were sinners, that it was their right and duty to make war upon them wher-ever they could be found, and to make slaves of all they could take as Prisoners."*[9] Remembering this conversation when he became president, Jefferson sent a military force to North Africa in 1801, reasserting the right of free pas-sage for American ships, and adding the now-famous words to the Marine Corps Hymn: *"...to the shores of Tripoli."* Jefferson understood the dangerous nature of Islamic ideology evidenced in his time.

Present-day jihadist activity in America was ex-posed for the first time in Muslim Brotherhood docu-ments introduced as evidence in a 2008 trial in Dallas, Texas. The Holy Land Foundation was the largest Islamic charity in the United States until its leaders were convicted in federal court of funding terrorist organizations. Among the documents introduced in court was *An Explanatory Memorandum on the Strategic*

Goals for the Group in North America detailing the Muslim Brotherhood's strategy for America.

> *The process of settlement is a "Civilization-Jihadist Process" with all the word means. The Ikhwan (brothers) must understand that their work in America is a kind of grand Jihad in eliminating and destroying the Western civilization from within and "sabotaging" its miserable house by their hands and the hands of believers so that it is eliminated and God's religion is made victorious over all other religions.* [10]

This organization could not have given a clearer and more specific statement of its malicious intent to undo and replace America's culture and political establishment with Islam's system of theocratic control. By inference it is also clear that the Brotherhood will use whatever means necessary for however long as it might take to bring about its concept of victory.

In the United States there is currently a population of 3.3 million Muslims, which is projected to reach 8 million by 2050.[11] Worldwide Muslims represent the fastest growing religion, numbering 1.6 billion in 2010.[12] Fortunately, most of these individuals are not committed to active jihad and do not adhere to the teachings of

Sayyid Qutb and the Muslim Brotherhood. Many sincerely believe Islam to be a religion of peace. However, it is a fact that *some* do believe in militant jihad and *any* percentage of a billion is a large number. Alarmingly, we don't know what that number is.

In the United States various organizations have been founded since the 1950s under the umbrella of the Brotherhood, such as the Council on American Islamic Relations (CAIR), the Islamic Society of North America (ISNA), and Muslim Students Associations (MSA).[13] It would be reasonable to assume that these organizations have the same aims as their parent. A Middle East expert defined these aims as *"advocating Islam as a political as well as a religious system...(requiring) elimination of all non-Islamic influences in social, political, economic, and military spheres of life."*[14]

There are many Islamist terrorist groups operating around the world with the same aims as the Muslim Brotherhood. These include Hamas, Al Qaeda, the Islamic State (ISIS), Boko Haram, the Taliban, and many more. Hamas was specifically organized by the Muslim Brotherhood, and although the connection between the Brotherhood and ISIS is not clear, their aims are the same: to establish a worldwide caliphate under shari'a law. All these terrorist groups operate in a highly visible, violent manner across the Middle East and Africa and increasingly worldwide. Most Muslim Brotherhood organizations operate by more subtle means but with the same ultimate goal of global jihad.[15]

True Believers

Members of the Muslim Brotherhood and other jihadist organizations believe in the cause of Islamic jihad that stimulates a long-term effort and unbelievable sacrifice on the part of thousands (and possibly millions). We see men, women, and children indoctrinated in the belief that, in furtherance of this cause, they are assured of a place in paradise when they forfeit their own lives. They also believe that they are compelled by their religion to bring death to those outside the faith. Death and destruction are necessary to cause fear, to weaken the belief of others, to demonstrate power, and to thereby bring the world of unbelievers into submission to Islam.

Another of the important Muslim Brotherhood ideologues, Abdullah Azzam, wrote *Martyrs: The Building Blocks of Nations*, a work considered foundational for global jihad in this century. In it he states: *"Indeed nations are only brought to life by their beliefs and their concepts and they die only with their desires and their lusts."*[16] Those who proclaim themselves our enemies are focused intensely on the realm of belief. When we become preoccupied with the material aspects of our culture and ignore those ideals of lasting value that we should stand for, we do so at our own peril.

1   Raymond Ibrahim, "The Muslim Brotherhood," *Front Page Magazine*, August 27, 2013, accessed July 28, 2016, http://www.frontpagemag.com/fpm/202247/muslim-brotherhood-origins-efficacy-and-reach-raymond-ibrahim.

2   Omar Sacirbey, "The Muslim Brotherhood's 'Intellectual Godfather,'" *The Washington Post*, February 12, 2011, accessed July 28, 2016, http://www.washingtonpost.com/wp-dyn/content/article/2011/02/11/AR2011021106019_pf.html.

3   Ibrahim, "The Muslim Brotherhood."

4   Sacirbey, "The Muslim Brotherhood's 'Intellectual Godfather.'"

5   Sayyid Qutb, *Milestones* (1964; repr., New Delhi: Islamic Book Service, Ltd. 2015), 76.

6   Ibid., 9–11.

7   Ibid.

8   Ibid., 75, 158. These interpretations of the Meccan and Medinan periods are further explained by Manzar Zaidi, at: Manzar Zaidi, "A Taxonomy of Jihad," *Arab Studies Quarterly* 31, no. 3 (2009): 21–34. *Military & Government Collection*, EBSCOhost, accessed September 16, 2016.

9   Joseph Carducci, Downtrend.com. *Interesting Look Back at First American War against Islam*, accessed August 6, 2016, http://downtrend.com/jrc410/interesting-look-back-at-first-american-war-against-islam.

10   John Guandolo, *Raising a Jihadi Generation* (Vienna, VA: Lepanto Publishing, 2013), 19; Lorenzo Vidino, *The New Muslim Brotherhood in the West* (New York: Columbia University Press, 2010), 171–2.

11   Besheer Mohamed, *A New Estimate of the U. S. Muslim Population*, Pew Research Center, accessed September 21, 2016, http://www.pewresearch.org/fact-tank/2016/01/06/a-new-estimate-of-the-u-s-muslim-population/.

12   Michael Lipka, *Muslims and Islam: Key Findings*, Pew Research Center, July 22, 2016, accessed July 29, 2016, http://www.pewresearch.org/fact-tank/2016/07/22/muslims-and-islam-key-findings-in-the-u-s-and-around-the-world/.

13   From evidence admitted in the Holy Land Foundation trial as analyzed by John Guandolo and Lorenzo Vidino (see Bibliography), showing proof of these associations.

14   Youssef H. Abouel-Enein, *Militant Islamist Ideology: Understanding the Global Threat* (Annapolis, MD: Naval Institute Press, 2010), 2. Commander Aboul-Enein is a Naval of-

ficer, Middle East Foreign Officer, and Chair of Islamic Studies at the National Defense University.

15 Ibid.

16 Abdullah Azzam, *Building Blocks of Nations*, accessed October 21, 2016, http://www.ummah.com/forum/showthread.php?128661-Martyrs-The-Building-Blocks-of-Nations-Sheikh-Abdullah-Azzam.

CHAPTER 2

The American Vision

Who's Who in America?

There are many Americans who know what they stand for, even though they may not have thought of it consciously. They are the patriots who love their nation, respect the flag, stand for the National Anthem, and proudly proclaim the Pledge of Allegiance. They include most of those who wear or have worn a military or first responder uniform in service to America. They often include those who are politically conservative. They should include every Christian, but Christianity today covers a broad spectrum of political belief as well as spiritual understanding. Whatever one's political or religious belief or group identity, a real appreciation of America requires knowledge about its history, founding, and unique form of government.

Unfortunately, there are Americans who have little understanding of or openly disavow what it means to be an American. They include many who are highly intelligent and well educated, influenced by trends in the modern culture, mainstream media, academic establishment, and entertainment industry. We also have professional athletes and other public figures that chose to use their moments in the national spotlight to "sit down" for America. These citizens have one thing in common: They take for granted the nation that gives them the opportunity to express their opinions and air their grievances. And sadly, they often view their patriotic fellow citizens with suspicion.

The groups that I have described are vastly different in many ways and operate across a seemingly cavernous political divide. In spite of this, however, the obvious fact is that we are all Americans. There are issues we must face together as Americans. We may quarrel among ourselves politically and even culturally, but when threatened by an alien ideology, we must unite. Our national well-being and even our ultimate survival hinge on how we answer the question: What does *every* American stand for?

America's Christian Heritage

People knowledgeable about the founding of our nation have the answer to the question which I have posed. I believe this to be true because only by knowing our origins do we understand what has made America the unique nation that it is now. In 2009, President Barack Obama declared to the world that America is not a Christian nation, referring, I assume, to the fact that a wide range of religions are now practiced in this nation. He was ignoring, however, the Christian roots of America that determined the very nature of our society and government, and which created the conditions under which all these other religions now flourish.

Historians have often looked in wonder at the men who presided over the founding of America. Arthur Schlesinger observed, *"The contest with Britain begot in the course of a dozen years the most remarkable generation of public men in the history of the United States or perhaps of any other nation...an explanation of the phenomenon lies beyond the wit of the historian."*[1] Practically every one of these men was either Christian or member of a Christian family. Most were extremely well educated with a broad knowledge of philosophy, classical law and politics, and were well versed with the enlightenment ideas then gaining in importance. All seemed to respond to the emphasis on reason and the importance of free inquiry in science and religion. However, they had no difficulty incorporating reason and religious faith into their own lives. All showed a deep reverence for God, although several developed their own antipathies toward the religious organizations of the time.

This unique group of men was able to integrate classical learning and modern concepts of philosophy with their own spiritual convictions and common sense. Reflecting the population at large, fifty one of the fifty five delegates to the Constitutional Convention were Christians, involved with Christian churches.[2] Although the depth of their faith in some cases cannot be determined, their understanding of God, creation, and human nature were largely influenced by the Bible and their Christian background. They brought this understanding to bear in the creation of the new nation.

Ultimate Authority in America

On July 4, 1776, our founding fathers took a step of faith into a great unknown. On that day this gifted group of men moved to cut the ties of royal authority with Great Britain, representing the basis of everything they knew: their property rights, monetary system, legal structure, economic activity, and underlying culture. As they severed this relationship, they sought a source of greater authority. At this pivotal moment, they purposefully turned to God, the supreme authority of all. Thomas Jefferson's immortal words from the Declaration of Independence state:

> *We hold these truths to be self-evident, that all men are created equal, that they are endowed by* their creator *with certain unalienable rights, that among these are life, liberty, and pursuit of happiness.*

When independence was voted, Samuel Adams rose in the Congress to exclaim: *"We have this day restored the* sovereign, *to whom alone men ought to be obedient."*[3] Alexander Hamilton said:

> *The sacred rights of mankind are not to be rummaged for among old parchments or musty records. They are written, as with a sunbeam, in the whole volume of human nature, by the hand of divinity itself, and can never be erased or obscured by mortal power.*[4]

John Dickinson also said: *"Kings and Parliaments cannot give the rights essential to our happiness. We claim them from a higher source—from the King of kings, and Lord of all the earth. They are created in us by the decrees of Providence, which establish the laws of our nature."*[5]

At an early point in American history, the French diplomat and historian, Alexis de Tocqueville, traveled throughout the nation studying its institutions and people. Trying to determine the source of the young country's greatness, he considered the abundance of harbors, rivers, fertile fields, forests, mines, vast commerce, democratic government, and "matchless constitution." To some extent he found answers in all of these areas. However, he ultimately came back to a more basic advantage:

> *There is no country in the world where the Christian religion retains a greater influence over the souls of men than in America; and there can be no greater proof of its utility and of its conformity to human nature than that its influence is powerfully felt over the most enlightened and free nation of the earth.*[6]

---

1   Arthur Schlesinger, *The Birth of the Nation: A Portrait of the American People on the Eve of Independence* (Boston, MA: Houghton Mifflin Company, 1968), 245.
2   John Eidsmoe, "Obama: America Not a Christian Nation," *The New American*, accessed August 6, 2016, http://www.thenewamerican.com/usnews/politics/item/2576-obama-america-not-a-christian-nation.

3   Samuel Adams, An abridged version of "American Independence," August 1, 1776, accessed October 21, 2016, http://krfs.net/pdfs/TWWU110703a.pdf.

4   Alexander Hamilton, *The Constitution Reader,* accessed October 21, 2016, http://www.constitutionreader.com/debates/naturalrights.engz.

5   Bernard Bailyn, *The Ideological Origins of the American Revolution* (Cambridge, MA: The Belknap Press of Harvard University Press, 1967),187, quoting John Dickinson.

6   DeTocqueville, Alexis. *Democracy in America.* The Henry Reeve Text (New York: Alfred A. Knopf, 1966, first published in 1835), 303.

CHAPTER 3
The Individual Citizen in America

O ur founders declared that in the new nation the supreme authority would be God, who created human beings and bestowed unique characteristics and self-evident rights on each of them. It was understood therefore that the rights to life, liberty, and pursuit of happiness did not come from the government or other men, but from God. So, in the hierarchy of this new nation, at the top, there would not be a king or president or legislative body. Instead, the position of preeminence would be held by the individual citizen, the only entity that exists with the possibility of a relationship with God. The founders derived this view of mankind from scripture that was then almost universally understood: *"So God created man in his own image,"*[1] and *"He has also set eternity in the hearts of men."*[2]

For someone reading this book without a belief in God, this concept of God-given rights may be difficult to take seriously. If this is the case, the question follows: If God did not bestow our rights, then who did? If they were created by *men* they can be taken away by men. Thomas Jefferson wrote: *"God who gave us life gave us liberty. Can the liberties of a nation be secure when we have removed a conviction that these liberties are the gift of God?"*[3] Americans who believe in God are able to have supreme confidence in the *unalienable* nature of their rights. They will never give up those rights freely. The nonbeliever can at least concede that the founders of our nation were motivated by this belief and created a form of government based on this belief that still benefits every American as no other government has in history.

I believe that God's agenda in the founding of America comprised the issues of faith and freedom and that he favored this new nation then and on many other occasions in its history. However, God does not have a relationship with any nation, including America, but only with those individual human beings who turn to him and seek him. From the beginning, as a foundational principle, Americans have been blessed with the freedom to do this without coercion. As James Madison put it, the founders *"extinguished forever the ambitious hope of making laws for the human mind."*[4] Such freedom is, of course, in direct contradiction to the tenets of Islam requiring submission to religious authority, by force when necessary.

In America then it was up to the people themselves to establish a government that would reflect their values and protect their God-given rights. This elevation of the individual citizen and the protection of his or her rights were the distinguishing characteristics of the founding of America and have continued so throughout its history. This elevation of the individual American to such a position of preeminence has been an irritant to every collectivist, ultra-liberal politician and would-be-authoritarian ruler ever since and is the biggest obstacle to Islamic jihadists seeking to impose their religion and shari'a law by force or intimidation.

With this freedom of will, individual Americans have achieved amazing results, mostly benefitting mankind. Unfortunately, this freedom also allows human actions that are thoughtless and misguided. Some lament a decline in America's moral fiber, and many in the Muslim world even call America the Great Satan because of its negative influence on their culture. As a Christian father and grandfather, I sometimes agree with this complaint and wonder what is becoming of our nation. John Adams provided this word of caution: *"Our constitution was made for a moral and religious people. It is wholly inadequate for the government of any other."*[5]

In spite of the concerns which some Americans have for their own country, our Islamic foes need to be aware that most of the cultural negatives that they see about

America are created by Hollywood, the music industry, large segments of our media, and divisive politicians. They do not reflect the character of the vast majority of Americans. Individual American citizens have never been and will never be easy to control or manipulate. The ingrained bias toward individual responsibility and individual freedom is the essential ingredient of American character and has made this the greatest nation in history.

This then is the **First Great American Ideal.**

The dignity of the individual: American citizens will not be coerced in matters of conscience. They understand that their individual rights come from God and that government exists to protect those rights and to allow them to live freely within the bounds of law and ethics.

---

1   Genesis, 1:27.

2   Ecclesiastes, 3:11.

3   Thomas Jefferson, The Thomas Jefferson Foundation, Inc., "Quotations on the Jefferson Memorial," accessed October 21, 2016, https://www.monticello.org/site/jefferson/quotations-jefferson-memorial.

4   Merrill D. Peterson, ed. *James Madison: A Biography in His Own Words* (New York: Newsweek, 1974), 94–95.

5   John Adams, The John Adams Center, accessed on October 21, 2016, http://john-adamscenter.com/who-we-are/why-john-adams/

CHAPTER 4
Limited Government in America

O ur Christian founders were also aware of the less benign aspects of human nature. The Bible pulls no punches in describing the fallen nature of mankind and the difficulty of any individual living up to God's expectations, including most of the Bible's greatest heroes. The apostle Paul gave a stark picture: *"For all have sinned and fall short of the glory of God."*[1] Accepting the fact that all human beings, even Christians, try to do good but fall short, our founders were wary of placing too much power in the hands of any individual or group in government. Also their own history is one of resisting the tyrannical authority exercised over them by the British monarchy. The Constitutional Convention of 1787 was therefore an exercise in balancing power and restraint within the new government.

The resulting Constitution that emerged from that convention created a government that has functioned effectively for over two hundred years and has guided America to a position of greatness in the world. The founders laboriously gave birth to a republican form of government with elected representatives and clearly enumerated, limited powers. Within the federal government there were separate executive, legislative, and judicial branches with separate powers and checks and balances among them. The authority not specifically granted to the federal government was reserved to the states and to the people. Fundamental rights were enumerated that could not be overridden by majority vote of the legislature or presidential decree. The founders thereby achieved a new and unique balance between the legal authority of government and human freedom unlike anything seen before in history, incorporating the **Second Great American Ideal.**

Limited government: American government is elected by the people and exists for the people, with powers clearly defined, separated, and limited by our Constitution to guarantee the freedom and dignity of every individual citizen.

---

1   Romans, 3:23.

CHAPTER 5

Religion in America

Amazingly, our founding fathers believed in the dominion of God even while remaining highly suspicious of ecclesiastical authority. James Madison argued: *"During almost fifteen centuries has the legal establishment of Christianity been on trial. What has been its fruits? More or less in all places, pride and indolence in the Clergy, ignorance and servility in the laity; in both superstition, bigotry, and persecution. Enquire of the Teachers of Christianity for the ages in which it appeared in its greatest luster; those of every sect, point to the ages prior to its incorporation with Civil Policy."*[1]

To support this view, Madison and the other founders were also able to draw guidance directly from biblical sources. Jesus himself said, *"Give to Caesar what is Caesar's, and to God what is God's,"*[2] and *"My kingdom is not of this world."*[3] A distinguishing feature of American government was thereby established in the very beginning:

religion would not be part of government. As stated in the First Amendment to the Constitution: *"Congress shall make no law respecting an establishment of religion, or prohibiting the free exercise thereof."* The government would not establish an official religion for its citizens. God was the source of authority, but his will would not be interpreted or enforced by religious/political leaders; instead, his influence would come through the freely exercised consciences of individual citizens and elected officials.

In 1802 President Thomas Jefferson wrote a letter to a church group in Connecticut addressing their concerns about religious freedom within their state. Focusing strictly on the federal level, he reiterated the Establishment Clause of the First Amendment, then added the comment: *"...thus building a wall of separation between Church and State."*[4] The idea of such a wall goes beyond the Constitution itself and has been used by various groups to advocate total elimination of religious influence in public affairs. The resulting conflict continues between religious and atheistic groups. Although interpretations vary, the phrase "separation of church and state" has come into general use as the American model of the relationship between religion and government.

This separation of religion and government has enabled not only better government, but also the purer exercise of religion. This has been true for the simple reason that "faith" or "belief" is a meaningless term unless freely chosen by the individual. Our founders recognized that the idea of coercing human beings into a state of belief in God was a pointless and futile exercise and displeasing to God himself. In no other area is the contrast between American ideals and Islamic jihadism more evident.

These ideas about religion and government point to the **Third Great American Ideal.**

Separation of church and state:
American government has not and will not establish a religion. Those elected to political office are expected to bring their respective religious beliefs and moral consciences to bear on questions of state, always acting for the benefit of all.

---

1   James Madison, *Memorial and Remonstrance against Religious Assessments*, The Founders' Constitution, accessed October 21, 2016, http://press-pubs.uchicago.edu/founders/documents/amendI_religions43.html.

2   Matthew, 22:21.

3   John, 18:36.

4   Thomas Jefferson, Letter to the Danbury Baptist Association, http://www.usconstitution.net/jeffwall.html.

CHAPTER 6

Freedom in America

When asked what makes America great, most would respond with one word: freedom. When asked what they fought for, most veterans would reply with the same word. We know that America is blessed with a degree of freedom seldom seen in the world now or at any time in history. No ideal summarizes all the others so well. No other ideal stands in such stark contrast to the ideology of militant Islam. Submission to Allah is one thing, but submission to rule by religious leaders is simply another form of totalitarianism, with no input from the governed, no limits to power, and no exercise of human reason.

Every American is free to speak openly, to write critically, to demonstrate against authority, to choose a profession, to succeed brilliantly, or to fail miserably.

Underlying these rights is the freedom of conscience and the ability to pursue one's own understanding of the ultimate purpose and meaning of life—and to turn toward or away from God.

Freedom has been an important underlying theme in God's relationship with mankind and America due to the fact that faith is meaningless without the freedom to choose it. If God had wanted robots, he would have programmed humans to act only on his command. If he wanted to control our relationship with him, he would have appeared regularly to issue instructions. He does neither. Apparently, God considers the concept of a person's relationship to him, or faith in him, meaningless without the freedom to choose.

Unfortunately, political or religious freedom has been a rare condition in human history. Most of the founders believed that the most important event in history was Jesus Christ's coming into the world as a human being. However, even Jesus did not come as an all-powerful figure. Instead he took the form of a quiet spoken man and was often a servant to others. In accordance with his own design, God chose not to overpower mankind with forceful demonstrations of his presence or his will. Instead, he gave men and women the free will to live their own lives and to seek him or not. The founders honored this God-given freedom of conscience and did not try to control others in spiritual matters. The essential freedom of every American then, has been to think and dream for him or herself, and to seek one's own spiritual answers to the important questions of life.

In modern history America has provided the model of this freedom to the world. From the beginning freedom has been the distinguishing characteristic of America. Countless Americans have fought to win and to preserve the liberties that have always been so important to this nation. Every American should be infuriated to see radical Islamists who are responsive to no electorate or to any code of common decency attempting to erode these freedoms through fear. The desire for security is powerful and continues to grow as an important political issue in America today. In this war, however, every American must stand for freedom. We fight a totalitarian enemy when we resist the continuing political pressure to sacrifice our freedoms for safety.

Standing directly athwart the path of Islamic jihadism is the greatest and most powerful ideal conceived by God or mankind for the ordering of human affairs. No ideology of submission or control will ever prevail over an America committed to the God-given freedom enshrined in its Declaration of Independence and

Constitution. America will always stand strong under the banner of **The Fourth Great American Ideal.**

Freedom: Americans are free to think for themselves and to seek God and meaning in their lives without coercion. Each citizen is born free and guaranteed the God-given right to life, liberty, and the pursuit of his or her own happiness.

CHAPTER 7

What Does It Mean to Stand for Our Ideals?

S tanding up for our beliefs has many meanings. In the war against ISIS and Islamic terror in the Middle East, it means fighting, in a military sense. Our armed forces have been engaged in this war for decades and still are. They deserve every moral and material support that can be provided. If America is to commit to armed conflict, every citizen should be part of the sacrifice. Some form of universal service for young adults should be strongly considered. There should at least be some form of taxation on *every* citizen to pay for the military effort. Since World War II, our soldiers and their families have fought a series of undeclared wars with little commensurate impact on the average citizen. We should never send our young men and women abroad to shoulder the burden of our conflicts without commensurate sacrifice on the part of every citizen.

As we see every day, armed conflict is not only occurring in foreign lands. Terrorist cells are operating all across Europe and America and threaten with violence anywhere at any time. Our law enforcement system is second to none, but will never be able to completely stop the extremists who have no regard for their own lives or those of innocent civilians. Every citizen must consider him or herself as part of the law enforcement effort. The watchword has been proclaimed: "See something, say something." Suspicious activity in a public place or in one's own neighborhood should be noted and, when necessary, reported. Every person, young and old, needs a heightened awareness of their own surroundings and possible threats when in public. Even though gun ownership and self-defense are controversial subjects in many quarters, they become even more important to the safety of our communities. All should have the means to defend themselves and their homes.

The threat of violent terrorism is the clear and imminent danger that we see. However, the more insidious threat to the nation is the hidden, long-term effort that we don't see. An expert on the Muslim Brotherhood has explained the "radical flank effect," whereby the apparently peaceful arm of Islam relies on the violence of extremist groups to create a favorable climate for "cooperation" between the Brotherhood and the government.[1] The 9/11 attacks served this very purpose, as many Muslims with Brotherhood ties were brought into the inner circles of government with the expectation that they would aid in the fight against the "terrorists." This infiltration into our political and military infrastructure remains an ill-defined and little-understood subversive threat to our nation, as explained in detail by John Guandolo and Philip Haney in the books outlined in appendix II.

On the home front, inside and outside government, jihadists are quietly and secretly working to undermine and overthrow our way of life. America faced subversion of a similar nature from communist elements for decades after World War II. Many communists and communist sympathizers believed in doctrines that were antithetical to our form of government and worked secretly within our society.

Under the Smith Act of 1940, hundreds were apprehended and convicted of seeking to subvert and overthrow our government. At the forefront of these investigations were the House Un-American Activities Committee and Joseph McCarthy's Senate Government Operations Committee. Although the concerns of the nation at that time were valid, the actions of these congressional groups have been vilified over the years, usually by liberal groups and academicians. When Hollywood was investigated, the chorus of criticism grew even more intense. It is not hard to imagine where the outcry would come from if our government used the same methods to find and root out subversive activity today. We might wonder what our politicians are prepared to stand up for.

Are Islamic jihadists in America in violation of the Smith Act? The statute states:

> *Whoever, with intent to cause the overthrow or destruction of any such government, prints, publishes, edits, issues, circulates, sells, distributes, or publicly displays any written or printed matter advocating, advising, or teaching the duty, necessity, desirability, or propriety of overthrowing or destroying any government in the United States by force or violence, or attempts to do so; Shall be fined under this title or imprisoned not more than twenty years, or both*[2]

It is beyond my scope to make a case under this statute against the Muslim Brotherhood, its many spin-off organizations, and the individual Islamic jihadists living and working within our nation. Clearly, overthrowing by "force or violence" is the method of choice for many. Others may be more patient, even though their ultimate goals are the same. We see the nature of the problem in its more advanced stages in Europe today, where Islamic no-go zones have grown in major cities and overt violence is escalating. Law enforcement is of necessity focused on the criminal aspect of this terrorism. Meanwhile, the people themselves seem to have little understanding or resolve toward defending their respective cultures against the threats of a subversive ideology.

The American people must understand and become engaged in this fight, and in this fight our beliefs are of utmost importance. Education is critical. The focus of this book is on the ideals that make Americans great. The nature and extent of the threat also must be better understood. In addition to what has already been mentioned, appendix II to this book contains information about four books and their authors that will serve to more fully inform anyone of the nature of jihadism within our nation and abroad. If you only read one of these, read *Raising a Jihadi Generation* by John Guandolo, a former FBI expert on terrorism. This book is an easy-to-read personal resource and an ideal reference book for local law enforcement and political leaders. Every community needs to be aware of the threat that seems to be coming closer to home every day. The concern of individual citizens may be the only way to focus the attention of community leaders on what we are facing.

At this time, America, like Europe, is of necessity focused on law enforcement to prevent and punish violent terrorist activity. We argue over whether to call it "radical Islamic terrorism" or just plain "terrorism." It helps to name the enemy, but in neither case are we naming the larger and underlying enemy. America's true enemy is Islamic jihadism, that strain of Islam seeking to bring the entire world, including America, under submission to Islam and shari'a law. In some cases it is a violent strain evidenced by acts of terrorism. In others it is a more subtle effort to gradually build Islamic communities, establish mosques, gain political influence, and build strength to enable more overt efforts at a future time. Europe shows us that these efforts seem ultimately to include violence. Clearly this is not just a law enforcement issue. All free people must understand the threat growing around them and consider their individual roles in combatting it.

---

1   Lorenzo Vidino, *The New Muslim Brotherhood in the West* (New York: Columbia University Press, 2010), 209. Mr. Vidino has been a member of the Harvard faculty and Director of the Program on Extremism, Center for Cyber and Homeland Security, George Washington University.

2   18 U.S. Code 2385, https://www.law.cornell.edu/uscode/text/18/2385.

CHAPTER 8
The Role of the Muslim Community

I realize it is somewhat presumptuous to speak of a Muslim "community." There is as much variety of thought and practice within Islam as there is in any other religion. An expert on Islam sites studies showing that, *"Most Western Muslims can be categorized as 'cultural' or 'sociological' Muslims. They interpret their faith much as do most contemporary Westerners, particularly Europeans: as purely cultural, a family tradition and a source of identity, but not as the center of their lives."*[1] Even the religious and practicing Muslims who faithfully attend their mosques don't necessarily belong to organizations or associations of other Muslims. None of the Muslim groups mentioned in this book, including the Muslim Brotherhood, speaks for the majority of Muslim citizens in America.

In spite of this diversity, the question still must be asked: How do Muslim Americans view this conflict?

How many support jihad, either actively or passively? How many long for the authority of a caliphate and imposition of shari'a law? Even though the vast majority of Muslims are not violent and are not our enemies, where do they stand on these issues? There is a fundamental conflict between loyalty to the Constitution of the United States and loyalty to any other legal system. Is our devotion to religious freedom being used against us by people devoted to a different system of religious and political laws? I can only ask these questions, because the implications are vast. Anyone who actively or passively supports those devoted to bringing into existence a different form of government is a threat to our nation.

I believe the Muslim community has a large role to play in addressing this problem. I am convinced that most of them are loyal citizens, happy to practice their religion personally and without a political agenda. But how will average Americans know who are loyal fellow citizens and who are enemies? The Muslim community itself can best accomplish the task of identifying, marginalizing, and eventually purging this strain of Islam. If this can't be done by Muslims, and somehow the task falls on government, one can only envision a controversial and strife-ridden future of loyalty oaths and committees to investigate mosques and individual citizens about their beliefs. Some European political experts have prophesied civil war in European countries if this is even attempted by governmental authorities.

Loyal Muslim Americans must come to terms with this issue to determine for themselves where they stand regarding their commitment to the Constitution of the United States. I don't see how any group can consider themselves American while supporting another governmental system by thought, word, or deed. By definition, a loyal American must stand for the American form of government and the foundational principles that make America what it is.

---

1 Vidino, *The New Muslim Brotherhood in the West*, 10.

CHAPTER 9

The Role of the Christian Community

Is This a "Holy" War?

So far I have not emphasized Christianity in this conflict, for a reason. America is not in a holy war against Islam, and I don't want to overemphasize religion in the arguments I am making. I believe that all Americans have something to stand for in this struggle, without consideration of their religious beliefs. In our ever more secular culture, most Americans have difficulty characterizing what is happening as a "holy war," even as we see others declaring a religious/ideological war against us.

Unfortunately, Christians cannot afford this attitude. Christians are being killed and persecuted throughout the Middle East and many other places in the world. American Christians should stand up for them in every

43

way possible. Furthermore, why should we expect less in America? The Muslim Brotherhood's plan for America moves forward in stages, depending on the size of their population in relation to the rest of the nation. As they grow stronger, they will grow more aggressive in establishing shari'a law until they can begin demanding submission from other religious groups, especially Christians and Jews. Under such duress what will *Christians* stand for? Hopefully, each will take seriously God's word: *"If you do not stand firm in your faith, you will not stand at all."*[1] The Christian's faith and answer to the question should be simple and unequivocal: *"I stand for the gospel of Jesus Christ."*

The Christian Community

Christians also have a clear role in bringing peace to this conflict. They have been blessed by their freedom as Americans to follow their religious beliefs according to their own conscience. They also know that they have a message of peace and hope to share with a troubled nation and world. They know that, not only has God given the freedom, but he has also provided the amazing and simple way for each person to find him in this life. Christians know that the way is through his son, Jesus

Christ. Jesus's simple message of forgiveness and reconciliation opens the way to the ultimate freedom to which human beings can aspire, a personal and intimate relationship with God, both now and in the eternal future. Christians have the opportunity to share this message. To the extent they are successful, our nation will benefit from a more God-centered culture and the personal and civic peace that comes with it.

Beyond this simple and straightforward purpose, Christians also have a role to play in American society as citizens of the republic. Every citizen, including Christians, should participate in the political process and work for a safe and prosperous nation in every way possible. As citizens, Christians should form their opinions and take appropriate action on important issues affecting their communities and the nation. They should stand up for America's foundational principles on any and every occasion. There is no conflict between Christian service and defense of American ideals.

However, the lessons of our own founding need to be remembered. Any religious group is on dangerous ground when it seeks power through the political process, no matter how worthy the cause. Our founders were wary of the Church wielding political power, just as we now see the evils of "political" Islam. Again, Jesus himself reminded all of us: "My kingdom is not of this world."[2] Christians only make their primary duty more difficult to accomplish if they are perceived as trying to coerce others in matters of conscience.

Christians can be most confident that they are doing God's work when they focus on the human level. They attract nonbelievers to God by demonstrating the joy, purpose, and peace that permeate their own lives and churches. This process is most effective when undertaken personally and with humility. I believe that God waits to see how well his followers will accomplish this duty. He also waits to see what nonbelievers will do with the freedom and opportunity that he has given each to respond.

---

1   Isaiah, 77:9.
2   John, 18:36.

CHAPTER 10
The Role of Every American

America is not at war with Islam. However, we are at war with a broad, undetermined segment of Muslim believers who are opposed to our way of life and system of government. This war has gone on for a long time and may go on for generations. Our enemies are growing in strength and determination and have proven that they will never negotiate a truce. In this war every American is a soldier. There can be no conscientious objectors or draft dodgers. No one stays home while the "boys" go off to do the fighting. The fight has already come here and will keep coming, in the form of terrorism and subversion. Our heroes have always been our military men and women and first responders. More and more they will be ordinary Americans who know what they believe in and who have the moral courage to stand up for those beliefs. I hope and pray that there are enough Americans willing and able to answer this call.

Americans must know what they believe in. This should not be difficult for Christians who understand America's Christian history. For those who are not Christians, the thought process should be the same. Our forefathers brought forth a nation and a government based on deeply held religious principles. This nation and government are based on those principles and have proven the most effective in history. All Americans should be able to freely pledge support to their nation and stand by her against all enemies.

The acclaimed novelist Pat Conroy was a Vietnam War protester in the 1960s. Later in life, reflecting on all he had learned about the world and his own country, he made a moving confession: *"I have come to revere words like 'democracy' and 'freedom,' the right to vote, the incomprehensibly beautiful origins of my country, and the grandeur of the extraordinary vision of the founding fathers. Do I see America's flaws? Of course I do. But I can now honor her basic, incorruptible virtues...I have come to a conclusion about my country that I knew then in my bones, but lacked the courage to act on: America is a good enough country to die for even when she is wrong."*[2] And how much more is America worthy of such devotion when she clearly stands for what is right?

In looking at another turbulent time in history, the historians Will and Ariel Durant eloquently concluded: *"So we end as we began, by perceiving that it was the philosophers and the theologians, not the warriors and diplomats, who were fighting the crucial battle of the eighteenth century."*[1] Our crucial battle today is also in the realm of ideas and belief. Philosophy and religion were foundational at the beginning of our history, and are even more important now.

Regardless of one's religion or politics, it should be evident that American history reveals truths about the nature of our nation that stand in stark contrast to the ideology of Islamic jihadism. Every citizen should know and appreciate the ideals that flow from these truths that define their country. Our history shows us the ideals that are uniquely American and that every American should be prepared to stand for and fight for if necessary:

The dignity of the individual: American citizens will not be coerced in matters of conscience. They understand that their individual rights come from God and that government exists to protect those rights and to allow them to live freely within the bounds of law and ethics.

Limited **government:** American government is elected by the people and exists for the people, with powers clearly defined, separated, and limited by our Constitution—to guarantee the freedom and dignity of every individual citizen.

Separation of church and state: American government has not and will not establish a religion. Those elected to serve are expected to bring their respective religious beliefs and moral consciences to bear on questions of state, always acting for the benefit of all.

Freedom: Americans are free to think for themselves and to seek God and meaning in their lives without coercion. Each citizen is born free and guaranteed the God-given right to life, liberty, and the pursuit of his or her own happiness.

My purpose in explaining the history and transcendent nature of these ideals is to give my fellow citizens positive reasons to believe in and stand for their nation. It is equally important to understand the threat posed by an ideology that is antagonistic to every one of these values. Islamic jihadists have a long-range plan to Islamize

America and the patience to pursue that plan for as long as it takes. The only counter to such a threat is an educated American public that understands and opposes this enemy and their evil ideology.

We often hear public figures end their speeches with, "God bless America." I sometimes wonder how much thought they give to what they are saying. "God bless America" is not a statement of fact, but rather is meant to be a *plea* to God. Christians believe that God has blessed America in the past due to the faithfulness of her citizens. We pray today that this faithfulness will continue and grow, and that God will continue to find America worthy of his favor. We may wonder if God is on our side in the present conflict. When asked this question during another war, Abraham Lincoln answered: *"Sir, my concern is not whether God is on our side; my greatest concern is to be on God's side."*[3] And to that, we can only say, *amen*, and pray, *God, bless America.*

---

1   Pat Conroy, *My Losing Season* (New York: Bantam Books, 2002), 375–6.

2   Will Durant, and Ariel Durant, *Rousseau and Revolution, 1715–1789,* Part X of *The Story of Civilization* (New York: Simon & Schuster, 1967), 784.

3   Abraham Lincoln Presidential Library and Museum Foundation, http://alplm. org/272viewessay.aspx?id=800.

APPENDIX I

Oath of Office for Federal Officials of the United States Government

Officials of the federal government, including the vice president of the United States, cabinet members, members of Congress, federal judges, federal employees, and officers of the military services do *not* pledge loyalty to the president, Congress, any political party, or any other organization. Instead they pledge their loyalty to the *Constitution of the United States*, as follows:

> **"I do solemnly swear that I will support and defend the *Constitution of the United States* against all enemies, foreign and domestic; that I will bear true faith and allegiance to the same; that I take this obligation freely, without any mental**

reservation or purpose of evasion; and that I will well and faithfully discharge the duties of the office on which I am about to enter. So help me God."

The president's oath is prescribed in the Constitution and also includes the words "protect and defend the Constitution of the United States."

Another important element of the oath is the embodiment of the sometimes less-than-obvious truth that our enemies can be foreign *or* domestic. At this point in history, America has both, and every American must be prepared to stand against both.

APPENDIX II

'Required' Reading

Raising a Jihadi Generation
by John Guandolo

R *aising a Jihadi Generation: Understanding the Muslim Brotherhood Movement in America* examines the history, writings and practical implementation of the Muslim Brotherhood's strategic plan to overthrow the United States and its impact on the security of all Americans at the local level. It focuses on tools for professionals in the law enforcement, intelligence, and military communities.

It must be understood that the Muslim Brotherhood in America prepares the ground for, supports, and facilitates jihadi operations. This handbook gives security and intelligence professionals a factual basis to address the enemy, changes what constitutes reasonable suspicion/probable cause, and transforms how this threat is approached and addressed. As this handbook makes clear, the Muslim Brotherhood has operatives in our federal law-enforcement and intelligence agencies, our military, but, most importantly, advising our senior leadership in our national-security apparatus.

This problem is much more one of counterintelligence and espionage than it is of counterterrorism. Once the control the Muslim Brotherhood has within the US government's decision-making process is understood, it becomes clear that America faces an insurgency inside our homeland that requires a very different response, especially from local law enforcement. In a counterinsurgency, the focus of the main effort is at the local level. Local police, working together with their local council, are the first line of defense against this enemy. But first there must be an educated and energized local populous. We face an enemy who is cunning, patient, well supported, and well organized. To underestimate this enemy is to lose the war.

John   Guandolo   is   the   founder   of UnderstandingTheThreat.com dedicated to providing strategic and operational threat-focused consultation, education, and training for federal, state, and local leadership and agencies. Mr. Guandolo is a 1989 graduate of the US Naval Academy who took a commission as an officer in the US Marine Corps. He served with Second Battalion Second Marines as an infantry platoon commander in combat operations Desert Shield/Storm, and at Second Force Reconnaissance Company for over four years. Mr. Guandolo was a combat diver, a military free-fall parachutist, and is a graduate of the US Army Ranger School.

In 1996, Mr. Guandolo left the Marine Corps and joined the Federal Bureau of Investigation (FBI), serving at the Washington Field Office. Shortly after 9/11, Mr. Guandolo began an assignment to the Counterterrorism Division of the FBI's Washington Field Office developing an expertise in the Muslim Brotherhood, Islamic Doctrine, and the global Islamic Movement. In 2006, Mr. Guandolo created and implemented the FBI's first Counterterrorism Training/Education Program focusing on the Muslim Brotherhood. He was designated a "subject matter expert" by FBI headquarters. For his efforts, in 2007 Mr. Guandolo was presented the "Defender of the Homeland" Award by US Senators John Kyl and Joseph Lieberman on behalf of the Center for Security Policy in Washington, DC. Mr. Guandolo served on the Washington Field Office SWAT team for over nine years, as its team leader for three of those years, and authored the standard operating procedures for the team.

After his FBI career, Mr. Guandolo worked for the Department of Defense conducting strategic analysis on the Global Islamic Movement. Mr. Guandolo advises governments—United States and others—on matters related to national security, specifically the threat from the Global Islamic Movement. He served as an adjunct instructor at the Joint Forces Staff College and the US Army War College. He is one of the authors of the *Shariah: The Threat to America*, the first comprehensive book on the threat from the Islamic Movement in the United States. He is a Claremont Institute Lincoln fellow, a senior fellow at the Centennial Institute, and a Knight of Malta. Mr. Guandolo frequently appears on television and radio, and regularly publishes articles related to these matters in a number of media outlets. His website is www.UnderstandingtheThreat.com.

Defeating Jihad: The Winnable War by Dr. Sebastian Gorka

Since September 11, 2001, America has been at war. And that's all anyone can say with certainty about a conflict that has cost seven thousand American lives and almost $2 trillion. Victory is impossible as long as the most basic strategic questions—Who is the enemy? Why are we fighting?—remain unanswered. Yet this war is eminently winnable if we remove our ideological blinders and apply basic strategic principles. That means accurately naming the enemy, understanding his plan, and drawing up a strategy to defeat him.

According to Dr. Sebastian Gorka, one of the most experienced and sought-after authorities on counterterrorism, our enemy is not "terror" or "violent extremism." Our enemy is the global jihadi movement, a modern totalitarian ideology rooted in the doctrines and martial history of Islam. America has defeated totalitarian enemies before. Providing a desperately needed dose of clarity, Dr. Gorka shows how we can do it again. He reveals how a toxic political agenda has corrupted our national-security practices, precluding the kind of clear-eyed threat analysis and strategic response that led to victory in the Cold War. In *Defeating Jihad* Dr. Gorka refers to formerly top-secret analyses that shaped the

US response to the communist threat, and produces a compelling profile of the jihadi movement—its mind and motivation—and a plan to defeat it.

Dr. Sebastian Gorka, PhD, serves as the Vice President and Professor of Strategy and Irregular Warfare at the Institute of World Politics in Washington, DC. Previously, he served as the Major General Matthew C. Horner Distinguished Chair of Military Theory at Marine Corps University where he provided courses and lectures on irregular warfare. He is an internationally recognized authority on issues of national security, irregular warfare, terrorism, and democratization and has testified before Congress and briefed the CIA, ODNI, NCTC, NIC, and the Commandant of the Marine Corps. His website, TheGorkaBriefing.com, is a collection of his national-security commentary and analysis. He served as a subject matter expert for the Office of the US Attorney in Boston for the Tsarnaev trial.

Dr. Gorka is an adjunct professor with USSOCOM's Joint Special Operations University where he serves as lead instructor for the Special Operations Combating Terrorism course, as well as the interagency and senior/executive counterterrorism courses. He is also an adjunct professor in national security at Georgetown University's McCourt School of Public Policy, and is a regular instructor with the US Army's Special Warfare Center and School in Fort Bragg and for the FBI's Counterterrorism Division.

He has published in excess of 140 monographs, book chapters, and articles, many for the JANES Group of the UK, and *Special Warfare,* the official publication of US Army Special Operations Command. Along with Dr. Chris Harmon and the late COL Nick Pratt (USMC), he was a contributor and coeditor of *Toward a Grand Strategy against Terrorism* (McGraw Hill). With Dr. David Kilcullen, he coauthored a study of Al Qaeda's use of strategic communications for the Praeger title, *Influence Warfare*. He serves on the Board of Advisors for the Council for Emerging National Security Affairs (CENSA).

Dr. Gorka holds a PhD in political science from Corvinus University in Budapest with his dissertation on "The Evolution of Terrorism: The Difference between Cold War Political Violence and Al Qaeda." He was a Kokkalis fellow at Harvard's J. F. Kennedy School of Government focusing on public policy and international security as well as an international research fellow at the NATO Defense College. He earned his master's degree in International Relations and Diplomacy at Budapest University and his bachelor's degree from the University of London. He was born in the UK to parents who escaped Communism during the Hungarian Revolution of 1956 and is fluent in Hungarian with working knowledge of German and French. In the UK, he served with 22 Company of the Intelligence and Security Group (V) of the British Territorial Army reserve but is now a proud American. He is married to Katharine Cornell Gorka, President of the Threat Knowledge Group as well as the Council on Global Security.

See Something Say Nothing: A Homeland Security Officer Exposes the Government's Submission to Jihad
by Philip Haney and Art Moore

One day after a prominent US Muslim leader reacted to the November 2015 Paris attacks with a declaration that the Islamic State, also known as ISIS, had nothing to do with Islam, President Obama made the same assertion. He went on to describe ISIS as "simply a network of killers who are brutalizing local populations." After 130 people were brutally slain and another 368 injured in a coordinated attack on Western soil that authorities say was organized with help from inside France's Muslim communities, many still described ISIS as "murderers without a coherent creed" or "nihilistic killers who want to tear things down." Who exactly is the enemy we face, not only in the Middle East but also within our borders?

When the Department of Homeland Security was founded in 2003, its stated purpose was "preventing terrorist attacks within the United States and reducing America's vulnerability to terrorism." The Bush administration's definition of the enemy as a tactic, terrorism, rather than a specific movement, proved consequential amid a culture of political correctness. By the time

President Obama took office, Muslim Brotherhood-linked leaders in the United States were forcing changes to national security policy and even being invited into the highest chambers of influence. A policy known as Countering Violent Extremism emerged, downplaying the threat of supremacist Islam as unrelated to the religion and just one among many violent ideological movements.

When recently retired DHS frontline officer and intelligence expert Philip Haney bravely tried to say something about the people and organizations that threatened the nation, his intelligence information was eliminated, and he was investigated by the very agency assigned to protect the country. The national campaign by the DHS to raise public awareness of terrorism and terrorism-related crime known as If You See Something, Say Something effectively has become If You See Something, Say Nothing. In *See Something, Say Nothing*, Haney, a charter member of DHS with previous experience in the Middle East, and coauthor Art Moore expose just how deeply the submission, denial, and deception run. Haney's insider, eyewitness account, supported by internal memos and documents, exposes a federal government capitulating to an enemy within and punishing those who reject its narrative.

Philip Haney studied Arabic culture and language while working as a scientist in the Middle East, before becoming a founding member of the Department of Homeland Security in 2002, where he worked as a Customs and Border Protection agriculture officer. After advancing to become an armed CBP officer, he served several tours of duty at the National Targeting Center near Washington, DC, where he quickly was promoted to its Advanced Targeting Team, an unprecedented accomplishment for an agent on temporary duty assignment. Officer Haney won numerous awards and commendations from his superiors for meticulously compiling information and producing actionable reports that led to the identification of hundreds of terrorists. He has specialized in Islamic theology and the strategy and tactics of the global Islamic movement. He retired in July 2015.

Art Moore is an editor for WND.com and its monthly magazine and book-publishing division. He entered the media world as a public-relations assistant for the Seattle Mariners and a sports correspondent for Associated Press Radio. Moore served for ten years in Eastern Europe with a Christian organization and earned a master's degree in communications from Wheaton

College. Before joining WND shortly after 9/11, he was a reporter for a daily newspaper and senior news writer for *Christianity Today* magazine.

Islam vs. the United States by
Nicholas F. Papanicolaou

This book examines the historical, Koranic, cultural, political, and all-conquering character of many of the followers of Islam. It also exposes the strategic plan of the Muslim Brotherhood for the United States, the as-yet-unfulfilled obligations of the Islamic States under the UN Charter, the Universal Declaration of Human Rights, and the Organization of the Islamic Conference and its fifty-six member states. It concludes with a direct analogy and historical precedent to controlling radical Islam today as an all-encompassing way of life—namely, the elimination of state Shintoism in Japan under the Potsdam Declaration of the Allies in 1945.

Nicholas Papanicolaou was born in 1949 in Athens, Greece. He was educated at Williston Academy in Easthampton, Massachusetts, where he graduated cum laude in 1967. He then earned a bachelor's degree in economics from Harvard University, where he graduated with advanced placement in 1970, and a master's degree in business administration from Columbia University in 1972. He holds a doctorate in theology from the Phoenix University of Theology International.

He was vice president of the Onassis Organization in New York in 1973–75, and then joined his family business interests in shipping and other investments. In 1983 he became controlling shareholder and cochairman of Aston Martin Lagonda in the United Kingdom, maker of the famous Aston Martin and Lagonda motor cars. Under his watch, the factory was reopened and the company was returned to profitability. It was subsequently being sold to Ford Motor Company.

He is a cofounder and cochairman of the World Public Forum "Dialogue of Civilizations." The WPF brings together each year on the island of Rhodes, Greece, some seven hundred important officials and representatives from more than sixty countries for four days of open and frank deliberations on cross-religious and cross-cultural issues. Representatives include heads of state, prime ministers, top religious leaders from all the major faiths, and university professors and academicians. Past attendees have included the presidents or prime ministers of Austria, the Czech Republic, Lithuania, Iran, Algeria, the Palestine Authority, India, Bangladesh, Russia, Yemen and government ministers from Israel, France, Greece, China, Indonesia, Kazakhstan, Malaysia, and other countries. He was awarded the Grand Cross of Saint Andrew of Russia for his work with the Dialogue of Civilizations.

Papanicolaou is also the Prince Grand Master of the Knights Hospitallers of the Sovereign Order of Saint John of Jerusalem, Knights of Malta, the Ecumenical Order.

APPENDIX III

'Optional' Reading

Readers interested in more in-depth informa-tion about the founding of America and the history of American ideals will find another of Larkin Spivey's books a valuable resource. *Miracles of the American Revolution: Divine Intervention and the Birth of the Republic* explains the ideas, the men, and the battles that led to American independence. For more information, go to www.larkinspivey.com. This book is available at Amazon.com.

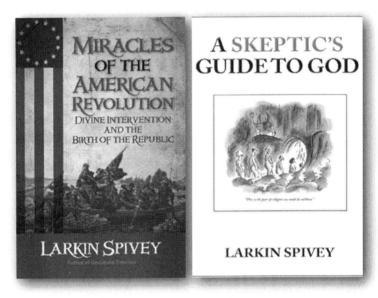

After reading *What Do We Stand For?*, a person who is not a Christian or has fallen away from Christianity may have some interest in investigating further the religion of his or her ancestors. Larkin Spivey was a religious skeptic for most of his life and has written this small book for fellow skeptics trying to answer life's hard questions by their own intellectual effort. *A Skeptic's Guide to God* can also be purchased at Amazon.com. More information is available at www.larkinspivey.com.

BIBLIOGRAPHY

Aboul-Enein, Youssef H. *Militant Islamist Ideology: Understanding the Global Threat*. Annapolis, MD: Naval Institute Press, 2010.

Armstrong, Karen. *The Battle for God*. New York: Alfred A. Knopf, 2000.

Bailyn, Bernard. *The Ideological Origins of the American Revolution*. Cambridge, MA: The Belknap Press of Harvard University Press, 1967.

Conroy, Pat. *My Losing Season*. New York: Bantam Books, 2002.

De Tocqueville, Alexis. *Democracy in America*. The Henry Reeve Text. New York: Alfred A. Knopf, 1966, first published in 1835.

Durant, Will, and Ariel Durant. *Rousseau and Revolution, 1715–1789*, Part X of *The Story of Civilization*. New York: Simon & Schuster, 1967.

Eidsmoe, John. *Christianity and the Constitution: The Faith of Our Founding Fathers.* Grand Rapids, MI: Baker Book House Company, 1987.

Gorka, Dr. Sebastian Gorka. *Defeating Jihad: The Winnable War.* Washington, DC: Regnery Publishing, 2016.

Guandolo, John. *Raising a Jihadi Generation.* Vienna, VA: Lepanto Publishing, 2013.

Haney, Philip, and Art Moore. *See Something Say Nothing: A Homeland Security Officer Exposes the Government's Submission to Jihad.* WND Books, 2016.

Lawrence, Bruce B. *Shattering the Myth: Islam beyond Violence.* Princeton, NJ: Princeton University Press, 1998.

Lewis, Bernard. *The Middle East: A Brief History of the Last 2,000 Years.* New York: Touchstone, 1995.

Lewis, Bernard. *What Went Wrong? The Clash between Islam and Modernity in the Middle East.* New York: Perennial, 2002.

Papanicolaou, Nicholas. *Islam vs. the United States.* Chambersburg, PA: GoingeBook, 2010.

Qutb, Sayyid. *Milestones.* 1964. Reprint, New Delhi: Islamic Book Service, Ltd, 2015.

Schlesinger, Arthur. *The Birth of the Nation: A Portrait of the American People on the Eve of Independence.* Boston, MA: Houghton Mifflin Company, 1968.

Vidino, Lorenzo. *The New Muslim Brotherhood in the West.* New York: Columbia University Press, 2010.

Wheatcroft, Andrew. *Infidels: A History of the Conflict between Christendom and Islam.* New York: Random House, 2005.

41197485R00053

Made in the USA
Middletown, DE
06 March 2017